Sorry Ya Got Dumped!

All rights reserved. No part of this book may be copied, reproduced, stored, or transmitted in any form or by any means—electronic, mechanical, photocopying, recording, or otherwise—without prior written permission from the author or publisher. Unauthorized use, distribution, or duplication of this material is strictly prohibited and may result in legal action.

This book is intended for entertainment and stress relief purposes only. The content within is not a substitute for professional medical, psychological, financial, or legal advice. If you are experiencing emotional distress, mental health struggles, or need guidance regarding your personal situation, please seek the support of a licensed professional.

All characters, scenarios, and references in this book are either fictional, humorous, or used for creative expression. Any similarities to real-life individuals, living or dead, are purely coincidental.

Copyright © [2026] G'Bryella Whyt
ISBN: [978-1-971419-13-8]
Published by [G'Bryella Whyt]
For permissions, inquiries, or rights-related matters,
contact: [gbryellwhyt@gmail.com]

Hello there, pretty girl, how do you do?
I'm a ghost sent down to get you through.

Breakups suck, and do you know why?
Because you picked the wrong f*cking guy.

I know you feel like you're gonna die,
But babe, you're not one of those girls
who look pretty when they cry.

NO SOBER TEXTING

Oh yeah, text him—what a genius plan!
Maybe beg a little? Be his biggest fan?

Put the phone down, show some respect for you,
Blowing up his phone won't make him want you.

Toss it, hide it, throw it away,
If he loved you, you wouldn't be single today.

NO DRUNK TEXTING

Oh yes, take shots and let the tears flow,
While you're out with your friends dressed like a ho.

Then text, "I miss you"—how tragic, how sweet,
Maybe he'll dump her and fall at your feet!

Put the drink down, don't hit send,
Drunk desperation won't bring him back, the end.

NO STALKING THEIR SOCIAL MEDIA

Go ahead, stalk him—let's play detective!
Maybe his posts hold some hidden perspective?

Zoom in, analyze, drive yourself mad,
Oh look, he's smiling—doesn't look sad.

Put the phone down, don't start to obsess,
He's not posting hints, he just couldn't care less.

NO COMPARING YOURSELF

Oh wow, she's so basic, you're hotter than that.
Or maybe she's stunning, and now you feel fat?

You zoom in, you judge, you spiral, you cry,
You have to accept he's no longer your guy.

Put the phone down, stop keeping score,
Get back on Tinder—just don't be a whore.

NO SLEEPING WITH THEM 'ONE MORE TIME'

Oh yes, great plan—one last screw,
A farewell ride to bid adieu.

You'll wake up hopeful, he'll run out the door,
He doesn't love you—he just wanted more.

Never sleep with an ex, not ever,
Unless you love regret—then sure, whatever.

NO ASKING FOR CLOSURE

Beg him to see you for closure—yeah, great plan,
He'll feed you some lies, just like every man.

He'll say, "It's not you, it's really just me,"
But spoiler alert—that's pure fantasy.

Closure is bullshit, we all know it's true,
Don't you want a guy begging to be with you?

NO STAYING IN BED FOR A WEEK

Oh yes, stay in bed, rot away in despair,
Maybe if you sulk long enough, he'll magically care!

Skip showers, eat junk, let your life fall apart,
That's definitely how you'll win back his heart.

Get up, get dressed, go touch some grass,
No man is worth looking this much like trash.

NO ROMANTICIZING THE RELATIONSHIP

Sometimes he was a great guy, we all know,
But he left you for a week, stranded with a broken toe.

He went to watch football while you were sick,
Those are the actions of an adolescent prick.

You don't miss him, you miss having a plus one,
Stop being dumb—you were miserable, hun.

NO TRYING TO MAKE THEM JEALOUS

Oh yes, post nonstop, make sure he sees,
Like desperation ever brought a man to his knees.

Jealousy works when they don't know a thing,
Not when you're online acting like a drama queen.

Go silent, disappear, let him sit and stew,
Maybe he'll wonder who's screwing you.

NO POSTING QUOTES

Stop posting quotes, it's painful to see,
"It's better to have loved and lost"? Girl, let it be.

You look unhinged, we're all concerned,
Even your ex thinks you've crashed and burned.

The "love yourself" posts? A new kind of low,
Even your cat thinks it's time to go.

NO GETTING A TATTOO!

You're in pain, you need a new start,
So you got "Warrior Goddess" inked on your heart.

A butterfly? A phoenix? His name on your thigh?!
Oh honey, that's regret in permanent dye.

The tattoo guy smiled, "Looks great, no doubt,"
Then whispered, "Damn, breakups really pay out."

NO CUTTING YOUR HAIR

Really? Bangs? What is wrong with you?
You wanna be heartbroken AND ugly too?!

Don't you ever wanna date another man?
Chopping your hair won't fix your plan.

Now you're single, sad, and look like a nun,
You went from a ten to a strong minus one.

NO REBOUND DATING

Oh wow, you're dating? That's so brave!
Too bad you're not ready and acting deranged.

You show up stunning, high heels, tight dress,
But ten minutes in—a full-blown hot mess.

You sipped your wine, all flirty and sweet,
Then ugly-cried into your spaghetti and meat.

NO VENTING

Wow, you're telling everyone the breakup news,
Boring the shoe lady while you're buying Jimmy Choo's.

You vented to a stranger in aisle three,
She abandoned her cart just to flee.

Your barista, your Uber, your therapist too,
They all wish you'd shut up and find someone new.

LISTEN

I'm sorry you got dumped — it happens, it's true,
But that says nothing about the greatness in you.

Healing takes time, you can't rush the pain,
But trust me — you will rise and love again.

You're special, you're strong, and deeply loved too —
Especially with Manolo right next to you.

Thank you so much for reading my book.
If it made you smile, laugh, feel seen, or just a little
less alone — please leave a review.
Your words matter more than you know.
And if you have any advice for women going through it, share it.
We all need each other.
Relationships are hard.
But what the world needs now, more than ever, is
women supporting women.
Let's keep lifting each other up, being honest,
and staying soft and strong at the same time.

With love,
– G

www.ingramcontent.com/pod-product-compliance
Lightning Source LLC
Chambersburg PA
CBHW041156120626
46547CB00020B/3234